The Splendour of
AUSTRALIA

*Autumn tints on the Tumut River,
New South Wales*

*Over: magnificent Millstream Falls,
south-west of Cairns, Queensland*

The Splendour of
AUSTRALIA

Robin Smith

VIKING O'NEIL

Timeless Land

This is no ordinary colossus. It is the oldest continent on earth; cradle of a people who, themselves, are many thousands of years older than any other human race.

The story of this land began near the dawn of time, 1 500 million years ago, when parts of present-day Australia emerged from the sea. Then, and at intervals thereafter, the skin of the land was alternately buckled into lofty mountain ranges and worn smooth again by wind and water.

Mainland Australia now lies evenly balanced above the scimitar sweep of the Great Australian Bight, carved by the restless Southern Ocean. To the north the fretwork edge of the continent is washed by the monsoonal Timor, Arafura and Coral Seas. To the west the land thrusts aggressively into the Indian Ocean, and to the east its boomerang-shaped backbone curves towards New Zealand, 1 931 kilometres away.

It is a land more than eleven times as big as Texas, bigger, in fact, than the U.S.A. below the 48th parallel, or nearly as big as Europe excluding Russia; an island 3 200 kilometres from head to heel and 4 000 kilometres across its girth. It is the only continent occupied by a single nation; it has never been invaded or torn by civil war.

The face of the land is ever-changing; its natural features almost bewildering in their diversity. Where else can one find a creation of such exquisitely delicate and varied form as the Great Barrier Reef?

In stunning contrast, the great monolith of Ayers Rock stands in isolation 335 metres high on a featureless plain in Central Australia. It dates back 230 million years, during which it has been furrowed, scalloped and pot-holed by winds and storms of its own making. Measuring nearly ten kilometres around, it is the biggest rock anywhere, and to see its terra-cotta hue deepening to a hell-red glow near sunset is to see one of the country's most awesome sights and to realize why the Aboriginals regard it as a sacred place of their 'Dreamtime'.

Consider the ancient glacial lakes of Tasmania, filled with sparkling, sapphire-clear, chilled water, with rugged mountain remnants, carved into cirques by the relentless grinding of a shield of ice; consider the snow-covered heights of Mount Kosciusko and other alpine peaks on the mainland; then turn to the almost endless tracts of gibber plains and sandy deserts of the interior. Here the surface bounces back the heat of a merciless sun in a vain effort to be rid of it, and desperate spinifex and other desert-adapted plants hold on week-by-week and month-by-month for the rain which comes only a few days in each generation.

To the east, in the shadow of the highlands, there are rivers, fed in places by melting snows, that flow rapidly to the coast on one side, and more sedately inland, to the west. The sinuous Murray-Darling river system meanders for 3 700 kilometres and is navigable for 1 450 kilometres; yet there are streams which appear on maps but rarely carry water and still more infrequently reach their destinations — streams which feed the world's most extensive artesian basin and about once in a lifetime prove themselves by flowing eighty to one hundred kilometres wide. In doing so they spread a thin sheet of water over the huge salt-pan, 240 kilometres long and eighty kilometres wide, that is shown on maps as Lake Eyre.

This is Australia — vast, ageless, sometimes pitiless and savage, frequently vital, often beautiful and fruitful, always colourful.

For the last sixty million years Australia has been isolated by surrounding seas and oceans, and as a result of this insular state its animal and plant forms have developed with a minimum of outside interference. Many creatures have evolved or found sanctuary here, cut off from evolutionary trends in other parts of the world.

Examples are not difficult to find. Apart

*River Red Gums, Flinders Range,
South Australia*

from the opossums and oppossum-rats of the North, Central and South Americas, there are no surviving marsupials outside Australia, which is home to more than one hundred species. The last of the marsupials which ranged from North America to Europe perished twenty-five million years ago. While mammals throughout the rest of the world have developed to the stage at which they give birth to young in fully-formed condition, the most characteristically Australian species continue to lay eggs (as is the case with the duck-billed platypus and the spiny anteater) or (as do kangaroos, possums and koalas) give birth to almost embryonic young which are nurtured in the female's pouch until they are old enough to fend for themselves.

Among the birds that are unique to Australia is the kookaburra, the world's largest kingfisher, which has forgotten how to fish; instead it has developed a palate for rodents and reptiles, and fills the forest with its 'laughing jackass' cries. Black swans are unknown anywhere else, and so are the forest-dwelling lyrebirds.

The giant wedge-tailed eagle, bird of paradise and the strange brolga or native companion, whose ceremonial dances have been incorporated in many Aboriginal dances and legends, have given individuality to Australia's fauna. So have frilled lizards and goannas, and termites that always build their blade-like hill homes facing north and south.

Like the mammals and birds, the plants of Australia have evolved in isolation for millions of years, and though some are related to plants in other parts of the world, many are unique. Certain types have flourished and increased their holding, like the myrtle family which is represented by more than 600 eucalypts and smaller flowering plants.

Grass-skirted 'black-boys', paunchy bottle-trees, stilt-legged pandanus palms, knobbly mangroves surrounded by spear-like shoots, desert she-oaks with leaves of delicate tracery — all give the Australian landscape its unique character.

Wattles or acacias, 600 species of them ranging from straggly bushes to small trees, also brighten the native bushland with their golden flowers. But for sheer colour, the myriads of seasonal wildflowers that carpet the ground in every State following spring and summer rains, are without equal. Western Australia has 6 000 different species, and every State has a host which is endemic to it.

Australia is so vast that much of it would remain unknown if it could not be explored vicariously, at leisure, through the media of books, paintings, films and photographic illustrations. In preparing this book, I have purposely avoided those scenes that show the impact that Australians have made on their country, the tremendous industrial development, ever-expanding and ever-present in the lives of the urban population. This is a book of the Australian countryside and coastline. You will see that this is not an endless expanse of semi-desert with stockmen riding the boundary fences, but one of infinite change. You will glimpse orderly green paddocks dotted with sheep, and seemingly limitless expanses of sienna-coloured landscape, palled in frightening stillness, stretched out beneath a tremendous sky. You will view mountains bathed in such a furnace-red light they look like heaps of near-molten metal; sheets of water thundering in headlong flight through forests of limitless greens; steel-grey cliffs locked in their endless struggle with the sea, and quiet havens guarding secluded beaches. You will also see sunburnt waterless gorges and placid landscapes with meandering rivers, chilling snowscapes, deep-blue tropical bays, giant gum-trees, great sweeping smooth stretches of sand, and mountains steeped in pastel-blue haze. All of these are Australia.

ROBIN SMITH

6

Rock reflections in Ormiston Gorge, Northern Territory

*Mt Warning landscape, northern
New South Wales*

The East

When the rock surfaces of the world were being buckled and faulted on a grand scale, a relatively slight movement over the continent of Australia created the eastern highlands known as the Great Dividing Range. These mountains, which stretch in a sweep from the tip of Cape York well into Victoria, catch most of the rain which falls on the continent; they are the birthplaces of the great river systems which are the life-blood of all hinterland settlement, and of the swifter-flowing streams which empty along the coast.

If geography is a nation's destiny, it is not surprising that the east coast, which was the cradle of European settlement, has remained the region of greatest population. Cook discovered it, charted it and spoke optimistically of its potential. Yet when the First Fleet, bringing convicts from Britain, arrived in Botany Bay nearly twenty years later in 1788, it seemed at first as if Cook and his companions had misjudged the promise of the country which now seemed so hostile to both the settler and his crops.

It was not until 1813 that a route was found through the Blue Mountains west of Sydney and the vast fertile grazing lands beyond were unlocked. These well-watered, well-drained pastures held the true wealth of the colony: from the new lands came wool, and for decades to come Australia rode on the sheep's back.

Wool no longer dominates Australia's economy to the extent that it once did, but the East remains the pasture of Australia: wheat, wool and irrigation crops in the Riverina; cattle and vines in the Hunter Vallet; beef, sugar and bananas in Queensland.

But if the East is pastures it is also mountains, rivers, cities and beaches.

In their southern section the eastern highlands rise to their highest: snow-capped Mount Kosciusko at 2 229 metres is the tallest peak on the continent, and the surrounding slopes of the Snowy Mountains offer world-class skiing in winter. Here Nature, with more than a little help from Man, has provided Australia's greatest water catchments, now harnessed to generate electricity and irrigate thousands of square kilometres.

The Great Dividing Range is like a chain with missing links; in places it subsides into the landscape almost without trace, only to emerge again within a few hundred kilometres as a sharp outline on the horizon.

Each segment of the chain has its own distinctive terrain. The Blue Mountains, for instance, west of Sydney, are a breathtaking maze of canyons and sheer rock faces. Here the forest canopy is slashed abruptly by river valleys walled by high sandstone faces, and the changing light of day paints the landscape in varying hues of blue, green, mauve and purple. The Warrumbungles of New England are renowned for their strange rock formations — soaring knife-edged spires shooting up abruptly from the surrounding eroded hills; the Glasshouse Mountains, eighty kilometres north of Brisbane, are like the landscape of another planet — eight towering cones of rock, the legacy of a past volcanic era.

On the narrow strip between the mountains and the coast are the cities and towns of the eastern seabord, and here, on the very edge of this vast continent, the majority of Australians live.

Sydney, the capital of New South Wales and Australia's largest city, is built around one of the world's finest harbours — 290 kilometres of rocky foreshore twisted into a ragged coastline forms numerous small beaches, coves, bays and headlands. At weekends, merchantmen, ferries and hydrofoils mingle with a flood of pleasure craft and yachts which spread their white sails and multi-coloured spinnakers over the deep blue waters. Flanking the harbour entrance, the rollers of the Pacific Ocean crash on to rocky cliffs and beaches of golden sand; Sydney has some of the most popular surf beaches on the east coast and the east coast has the best surfing beaches in Australia.

Beyond the coastal mountains, great rivers and golden plains

Home to nearly three million people, Australia's oldest city is one of contrasts. Towering commercial buildings and apartment blocks thrust their way into the city skyline while in the foreground, the white sails of the Opera House on Bennelong Point vie for attention with the once-dominant hump of the Harbour Bridge. Yet amid the jungle of commercial office towers there are still many examples of the dignified architecture of colonial Georgian and Victorian styles.

Brisbane, the capital of Queensland, has retained a more provincial flavour; spread across the Brisbane River a few kilometres inland from Moreton Bay, it is a city of trees — frangipanis, poincianas, jacarandas, poinsettias, buckinghamias, bauhinias, coral trees and flame trees. The architecture is turn-of-the-century, with many shady wooden verandahs appropriate to the semi-tropical climate.

By contrast, the new cities of the Gold Coast, about seventy kilometres to the south, are a 20th century creation. Here, along thirty kilometres of Pacific beaches stretching from Southport to the New South Wales border, the resorts of Surfer's Paradise, Broadbeach, Burleigh, Kirra, Palm Beach, Currumbin, Miami, Greenmount and Coolangatta have fused into a ribbon conglomeration that is the City of the Gold Coast.

The Gold Coast is Australia's Miami, Waikiki and Riviera. Dazzling sandy beaches run for kilometre after kilometre between the ocean and the foreshore with its galaxy of flashing signs advertising motels, tall apartment blocks and luxury hotels. It is a winter haven for tourists from southern States and, in many senses, the playground of the East.

On the western side of the Great Divide stretch vast inland plains and river valleys where major rivers like the Murrumbidgee, Lachlan and Darling thread their way across the countryside providing water for huge areas of crop and pastureland. Bourke, on the Darling River 796 kilometres north-west of Sydney, is an old river town which is now a large pastoral centre and the world's largest railhead for wool. But in this country there are more acres than people, and away from the river and its surrounding irrigated pastures the land becomes dry, isolated and formidable. This section of the central north of New South Wales is often called 'back 'o Bourke', and beyond the 'back 'o Bourke' there is only the 'dead heart' of Australia.

Like most of Australia, the East has few major inland cities. West of the Darling River, not far from the South Australian border, is the large mining centre of Broken Hill, often called 'the Silver City' because of the immense lode of silver-lead-zinc mined there. Virtually isolated from the rest of New South Wales, it runs its own affairs with aggressive independence.

By contrast, Canberra, 300 kilometres inland from Sydney, is largely a city of government employees. Created early this century to serve as the national capital, Canberra, by reason of its significance and political influence, is usually regarded as the 'third city' of the East.

At the time of Federation in 1901, there was rivalry between the States over the siting of the capital. The dilemma was solved by setting aside a tract of land in south-eastern New South Wales which, together with another small area on the coast at Jervis Bay, was established as the Australian Capital Territory.

Since then, a striking 20th century city has grown on the sheep pastures flanking the broad shallow valley of the Molonglo River. The first isolated buildings have given way to a consciously-planned city of fine modern buildings which reflect the designs of architects of vision. Laid out geometrically, in circles, hexagonals, oblongs and ellipses, it is a clean and spacious city, without slums or the need for heavy industry. Lake Burley Griffin, named after the city's planner, is the centrepiece of the capital, and a counterpoint to the major buildings sited around its perimeter.

*Adelong landscape, near the
Tumut River,
New South Wales*

**Tweed River and Mt Warning,
New South Wales**

The 1 158-metre peak of Mt Warning
dominates the Tweed River landscape in
north-eastern New South Wales. The
summit, surrounded by rain forest, was
named by Captain Cook as a reminder of
rocks close to Tweed Heads. Some of the
most gentle and classically pastoral scenery
in Australia is to be found here on the
border of New South Wales and Queensland
in the Tweed River district. The land
produces sugar and tropical fruit, grown on
farms cut out of the forest. Valuable timber
is still to be found in the mist-filled valleys
of the ranges.

**Orara River at Coramba,
New South Wales**

The Orara River runs north and joins the
Clarence River upstream from Grafton. The
stream is swelled by the water of many
tributaries as it flows through the undulating
countryside. Agriculturally, the area is
productive, with dairying, mixed farming,
peanut and potato-growing the main
farming activities. The settlement of this
region began after 1838, when a pioneer,
John Small, made the first cedar cut.
Hardwood timber-cutting is still one of the
main industries.

14

Fitzroy Falls near Mossvale,
New South Wales

In the Southern Highlands about 130
kilometres south-west of Sydney, the Fitzroy
Falls cascade over a sheer rock face and
drop dramatically to the rocky gorge below.
Only five minutes' walk from the deafening
thunder of the waterfall, the bush resumes
its still silence and forest giants tower above
damp, fern-covered slopes. The area was
settled as far back as 1853 and many
historically interesting buildings can be seen
at the nearby town of Mossvale and along
the road which winds steeply down the side
of the mountains on its way to the coast.

The Three Sisters, Blue Mountains,
New South Wales

The Blue Mountains are, from a distance,
an intense cobalt blue. Spectacular
sandstone precipices ring the densely
wooded valleys and the rugged terrain is
broken by deep gorges. The Three Sisters at
Katoomba are the best-known landmark of
the mountains. These remarkable towers of
weathered sandstone rise more than 457
metres above their talus slopes in the
Jamieson Valley, 97 kilometres west of
Sydney. It took the first settlers a quarter of
a century to find a way over these ramparts
to the fertile western plains of Bathurst and
beyond.

Gerringong Beach and landscape, New South Wales

The small settlement of Gerringong is about 40 kilometres south of the industrial city of Wollongong and near the mouth of the Shoalhaven River. Although the area supports dairying and intensive cultivation and is primarily agricultural in character, the undulating paddocks slope down to a beautiful stretch of white sand and Gerringong has become a seaside resort where fishing is popular. There are many such little towns along the east coast which have grown into holiday centres as more and more Australians seek the relaxation of sea sports.

Rock fishing at Bermagui, New South Wales

Bermagui is a small town on the southern section of the New South Wales coast which is well known as a big-game fishing resort. The waters of the continental shelf at this point abound with fish, and visitors can enjoy the thrill of reeling in Snapper, Tuna or Australian Salmon. The rocky, ocean coastline of Bermagui and the neighbouring coastal town of Eden can be treacherous for swimmers but provides splendid opportunities for the adventurous fisherman who likes casting from the rocks into a swirling sea.

Yachts on Sydney Harbour, New South Wales

The Harbour (officially named Port Jackson) is the focal point of Sydney. It is the busiest port in the South Pacific and has a fleet of ferries, supplemented by high-speed hydrofoils, which carries commuters between the city and the North Shore suburbs. Hundreds of private yachts shelter in its coves, and on fine days the deep blue waters are dotted with sails. The classic ocean yacht-race from Sydney to Hobart starts here each Christmas and harbour activity reaches its peak as every available craft turns out to farewell the fleet.

The National Library, Canberra, Australian Capital Territory *(Top)*

Canberra is a mini-metropolis of parks, gardens, plantations and neo-classical public buildings in precisely evaluated proportions. The National Library is a splendid recent example.

Sydney Harbour, Port Jackson, New South Wales *(Below)*

One of Sydney's most famous harbourside landmarks is the Opera House, rising in all its gleaming magnificence on Bennelong Point.

**Mts Beerwah and Coonowrin,
Glasshouse Mountains, Queensland**

Eighty kilometres from Brisbane a group of
ancient volcanoes called the Glasshouse
Mountains thrust their sharp heads above
forest and bushland. These dramatically
precipitous trachyte peaks of convoluted
spires, domes and pillars reminded Captain
Cook of the glass furnaces of his native
Yorkshire. The tallest of the eleven peaks is
Beerwah which shoots abruptly into the sky
for 556 metres from an undulating plain
which has in recent years been extensively
cultivated. The Glasshouse Mountains are
one of the best-known landmarks within
easy driving distance of Brisbane.

**Mt Lindesay in the MacPherson
Range, Queensland**

The MacPherson Range is covered by thick,
sub-tropical forests which have never been
damaged by severe bushfires. The range
contains many vivid flowering trees and is
host to more than 20 species of tree and
rock orchids. The deep canyons cut by
mountain streams have formed many
spectacular caves and waterfalls. Mt
Lindesay, near the New South Wales-
Queensland border, rises to a height of
1 239 metres. Like the Glasshouse
Mountains further north, it is part of an old
volcanic cone, the core of which has been
gradually exposed and eroded .

Warrumbungle National Park, New South Wales

Some of Australia's most spectacular scenery is contained in the 5 700 hectares of the Warrumbungle National Park, 32 kilometres west of Coonabarabran and 483 kilometres north-west of Sydney. This jagged knot of spires, domes and mesas is the remains of past volcanic eruptions. The cones and craters are long since gone, their softer ash cut away by the streams which now flow through the deep gorges and valleys of the park. In their place are curious landforms such as the remarkable outcrops shown here. From left: Belougery Spire; Crater Bluff and The Breadknife.

Purlingbrook Falls, Springbrook, Queensland

There are said to be more than 500 waterfalls of exquisite beauty in the great Lamington National Park. Here, amid the jungle lushness, many of the coastal rivers have their headwaters. They tumble from the Lamington Plateau of the MacPherson Range and race down to the Pacific Ocean in a series of filmy waterfalls. The Purlingbrook Falls are the most famous in the Springbrook National Park where, within a comparatively small area the scenery includes sheer cliffs, caves and waterfalls, with large trees forming a canopy over tree-fern glades and tropical vegetation.

Brisbane and the Brisbane River
Captain Cook Bridge, Brisbane

The Brisbane River rises in the Brisbane-Cooyar Range and winds through rich dairying and agricultural country to Moreton Bay. Nineteen kilometres from its mouth, it is straddled by Brisbane, Queensland's capital city. Brisbane matches its sunny, sub-tropical climate with an easy-going, almost provincial atmosphere. Vivid flowering trees like jacarandas and poincianas flourish in the mild climate and add distinction and colour to the city's suburbs and parklands.

Surfer's Paradise, Gold Coast, Queensland

Every year Surfer's Paradise attracts thousands of sun-seeking holiday-makers to its beaches and resort accommodation. Tens of millions of dollars have been invested during the last 20 years in the construction of hotels, apartments and amusement centres. Eighteen separate communities are administered as the City of Gold Coast, the centre of which is Surfer's Paradise, where rolling surf on the eastern seaboard is a contrast to the tranquillity of panoramic, man-made waterways of residential areas inland.

The Far North

Almost forty per cent of the Australian continent lies within the tropics, yet to most Australians the Far North is as remote as a foreign country. Settled and farmed at isolated points along the eastern and northern coasts, it remains essentially a vast empty space; in places teeming with animal and bird life, divided by great rivers and clothed in luxuriant vegetation, but almost everywhere oblivious of Man's presence.

Like so many parts of the continent, the variety of the landscape is enormous. Along the eastern and northern coasts, within the shadow of the monsoons, steamy jungle and warm wet grassland cover the land.

But as the monsoons dissipate southwards the landscape changes. Most of northern Australia above the Tropic of Capricorn is semi-arid grassland; something like one quarter is desert.

Where the rains fall the land is rich and fertile. On the moist coastal belt east of the Great Dividing Range, which runs the entire length of the State, sugar-cane is Queensland's major agricultural industry. The fresh green of the young cane crops covering kilometre after kilometre of the gently rolling country and flats along the coastal belt, with intermittent breaks of terra-cotta fallow ground, creates a distinctive landscape against a backdrop of mountains heavily forested on the landward side.

On a plateau between the headwaters of the Burdekin and Palmer rivers, west and south of Cairns, lies the volcanic soil of the Atherton and Evelyn Tablelands. This relatively isolated and sparsely-populated dairying and agricultural region has a beauty of its own, with outcrops of rocky hills and mountains, and rolling country bounded by areas of tropical jungle.

The coast north of Cairns includes some of the finest beaches and tropical seascapes to be found anywhere in Australia. At Buchan Point a striking coastal panorama opens up. Brilliant, sandy beaches stretch away in an uninterrupted view to Port Douglas, then beyond to the hazy outline of Cape Kimberley.

The road weaves in harmony with the shoreline, sometimes with a thin screen of palms or tropical vegetation, but mostly with open sand or rocky headlands on one side and steep, heavily forested mountain slopes on the other.

The central Queensland coast with its equable climate, and the north where the hot, humid weather is characterised by the monsoonal 'wet' between October and March, have their own particular attractions, but the coastal towns of Rockhampton, Mackay, Townsville and Cairns are seen by many tourists as jumping-off points for the islands of the Great Barrier Reef. The 'reef' which lies roughly parallel to Queensland's coast for 2 012 kilometres, is one of the world's most spectacular natural phenomena. Comprised of many thousands of individual reefs which form an almost unbroken chain, it is more varied than the jungles of the Amazon, bigger and brighter than the Grand Canyon.

The architects of this masterpiece of Nature are minute coral polyps which protect their soft bodies with an external skeleton of lime. How long did it take for these reefs to be built? The experts estimate thirty million years. Remains of even older, and now extinct, corals can still be found from Chillagoe in Queensland to the Gordon River in Tasmania. Some ancient corals date back 400 million years.

The Great Barrier Reef region covers about 207 200 square kilometres. In the south, off Gladstone, the reefs lie roughly 161 kilometres offshore, but near the head of Cape York Peninsula they are within about eleven kilometres of the land.

There are more than 300 kinds of coral and some of the most varied shapes and colours can be seen along the reefs outside the Whitsunday Group of islands.

The northernmost landmark of the Whitsunday Group is Hayman, an island which has become one of the most popular 'tropic-isle' resorts. Although it appears as a mere dot on the map a short distance off the Queensland coast near Proserpine north of

In the warm tropics, lush jungles, white beaches and coral seas

Brisbane, it has made a far-reaching impact on the Australian tourist industry. No longer does a holiday on a remote island mean living in discomfort for the privilege. When the islands of the Whitsunday Group were developed as tourist resorts, nothing was spared in the pursuit of comfort. Brampton, Lindeman and Pentecost are all islands which offer accommodation in idyllic settings amongst their palms, tropical trees, bougainvillaea and sapphire seas.

Many other tropical retreats are found in this northern section of Queensland and efforts are being made to preserve the natural beauty of these areas. Cape Hillsborough, near Mackay, is typical of nature reserves where the untouched tropical growth provides a refuge for the native birds and animals which normally abound in the hot, moist jungle.

The grasslands of Queensland and the northern portions of Western Australia and the Northern Territory are the principal beef-cattle areas of Australia, where giant properties sprawl across the landscape carrying herds of up to 70 000 head. Stations ranging in size from a few thousand to several hundred thousand hectares cover the land. They are so immense and so isolated that most have their own airstrip, workshops, schools and wireless transmitters. Some have their own planes, road-train units for moving cattle, and shops. From these vast rolling downs and plains comes a great percentage of Australia's wealth.

In the remote north-west of the continent, cattle stations and isolated settlements are sustained by major rivers: the Fitzroy flowing into King Sound on the Indian Ocean, the Ord, Daly and Victoria emptying into the Timor Sea. Between the Fitzroy and Ord river systems lies the Kimberley region, where the pioneering Durack family first raised cattle ninety years ago. And dotted on the largely blank map of the Far North are isolated settlements: Broome on the north-west coast, where men still go out in luggers to dive for pearls; Marble Bar to the south,

renowned for most of its existence as the hottest place on the continent; Wyndham near the mouth of the Ord, port for the cattle and cotton now grown by irrigation from the Ord River Scheme.

The northernmost city in Australia is Darwin, now being reconstructed after the disastrous cyclone of December 1974 virtually destroyed the city. Although regarded by some as more like a town than a city, it is the administrative capital of the Northern Territory and peopled to an even larger degree than Canberra by public servants. This tropical, free-wheeling, beery town is the only Australian community to have suffered major damage in war — it was heavily bombed and subsequently evacuated during the Second World War. It has a multi-racial population of Asians, Aboriginals and Europeans, and more than any other Australian city has a close racial affinity with its northern neighbours; residents of Darwin are fond of pointing out that they are closer to Djarkarta than they are to the Australian capital, Canberra.

Darwin is the starting point for crocodile, buffalo-hunting and fishing 'safaris' in the nearby coastal jungle, and for trips to the Arnhem Land Aboriginal reserve to the east, or to the Rum Jungle uranium mines, the sorghum project and the experimental farms around Humpty Doo station to the south. Its summers are humid and can be unpleasant, but the dry, hot winter season is delightful. Apart from the climate, tourists are attracted by the wildlife and vegetation, and by the mangrove and palm-fringed coastline deeply indented by the estuaries of large rivers.

Darwin is linked to the south, via Alice Springs, by the long bitumen ribbon of the Stuart Highway. The main centres on the road south are Katherine, 355 kilometres south of Darwin and Tennant Creek, 686 kilometres further down the highway.

Coral of the Great Barrier Reef, Queensland

This 2 012 kilometres long series of reefs is the largest coral conglomeration in the world, with many varieties of spectacularly beautiful coral, mostly submerged. The tiny coral-making creatures, called polyps, form colonies of different sizes, shapes and colours according to their species. About 350 kinds of coral have now been identified on the Barrier Reef — some of a soft, gelatinous texture, others extremely hard and spiny. Both hard and soft varieties may be of any colour from pure white through pastel tints of yellow, green and red to intense purples and rich browns.

Heron Island, a coral cay, Queensland

In the Capricorn Group of islands, 80 kilometres out from Gladstone on the Queensland coast lies Heron Island, a flat coral cay of about 16 hectares. Most of this area is a National Park; the remainder supports a thriving tourist trade. The island is formed of coral reefs and sand and rises no more than 2.5 metres above the sand, but it is covered by 12-metre high Pisonia forest and groves of Pandanus which contain many birds. The surrounding waters are rich in marine life and Queensland's first Marine Biological Research Station has been established here.

Daydream Island Resort, North Queensland

Daydream Island is one of a collection of islands in the magnificent Whitsunday Passage. It is a small island of volcanic rock and coral 5 kilometres from Shute Harbour. Lavish tropical vegetation and landscaped gardens surround the sophisticated Polynesian-style resort where life centres around the swimming pool. The free-form pool is large enough to have an exotic bar in the middle.

Pentecost Island from Lindeman Island, Queensland

These tropical islands form part of the Cumberland Group in the Great Barrier Reef, lying between Mackay and Bowen near the entrance to the Whitsunday Passage. Lindeman Island has an area of 16 square kilometres and is a tourist resort with an excellent airstrip. With the peak of Pentecost Island in the background the scene is one of tropical tranquillity. The tangle of dense bushy growth on the islands is edged with strips of near-white sand which contrast with the surrounding azure sea.

Tropical coastal scene, Port Douglas, Queensland

During the latter half of the last century, Port Douglas was the chief gold town of the north-east until the goldfields failed. Later, trade was lost to Cairns 64 kilometres south, where the railway terminated. Port Douglas is now the seaport for the town of Mossman and the surrounding district. The coastal north in this region is typified by flowering tropical trees and mountains rising out of the sea. The drive from Cairns to Port Douglas on a winding coastal road flanked by mountains and quiet bays must rank as one of the most pleasant experiences in Australian travel.

Palms and villa, Johnstone River, Queensland

Just south of Cairns and not far from the beautiful Millstream Falls, the North and South Johnstone Rivers form a junction at Innisfail, eight kilometres from where the combined tidal river enters the sea. George Dalrymple discovered the Johnstone River district in 1873 and eight years later the first sugar mill was built. Although crops of sugar cane and tropical fruit are the main feature of this coastal area, 30 kilometres inland from Innisfail is the Palmerston National Park which was established to preserve the jungle and rainforest vegetation.

South Johnstone landscape, Queensland

The sugar cane area of Australia is located along a 2 100 kilometre strip of the north-eastern coast, and almost all of the crop is grown in Queensland. The seasonal burning of the cane crops prior to harvest (to remove surplus foliage) is a spectacular sight, as crimson flames leap high against the black sky. The first cane in this area was planted as long ago as 1880, and now every year between June and December the population of nearby Innisfail is nearly doubled by the influx of cane-cutters.

Pioneer Valley from Eungella, Queensland

Tall palms and abundant undergrowth typify the vegetation of this area. The Pioneer River drains Eungella National Park, the largest mountain reserve in Queensland, and magnificent views can be gained from vantage points on a scenic road which crosses the valley. The Pioneer River was originally called the Mackay after John Mackay who discovered the valley in 1860. Today rich sugar cane and fruit farms have been established on the river flats 80 kilometres west of the town of Mackay, sugar capital of central Queensland, which stands at the river's mouth.

The south-west corner of Australia is perhaps 1 400 million years old. There was land here before there was life, even in the sea. With the Musgrave Range of Central Australia it is one of the oldest land surfaces on the face of the planet, part of a prehistoric land geologists call Yilgarnia.

The landscape of the south-west is rich in variety: the great forests of jarrah, karri and tingle-tingle, the hills near Albany, the Porongurup and Stirling Ranges are all found here.

The Aboriginal name Porongurup echoes the haunting chant of the native wind instrument, didgeridoo. Though only thirteen kilometres in length and about three across, the range is quite spectacular, for in places the 600-metre high granite peaks have been rent into blocks and slabs so sharp-edged and regular that they appear to have been cut by a knife. Some of these walls, like Castle Rock, tower hundreds of metres above the forested mountains at their base which, in turn, look down upon the plain far below, where sheep and cattle graze.

The Stirlings, like their near neighbours the Porongurups, rise abruptly from the surrounding plains, to give superb panoramic views. About 600 species of wildflowers (of which about thirty are peculiar to the area) bring a mass of colour in spring. Myrtles and banksias, heaths, wattles and red, yellow and pink mountain-bells are common; kangaroos roam the slopes, and more than 130 different species of birds add their song and colour.

The lofty karri trees of Western Australia are restricted to a small, high-rainfall area in the extreme south-west. Though not quite as tall as the mountain ash trees of Victoria, the tallest known specimens have been little short of ninety metres. They are the biggest trees in Western Australia, and higher than the tingle-tingles and jarrahs in the same area. The trunks of these trees may rise forty-five metres before any branches occur and their girth can reach twelve metres; a log thirty-three metres long from the

Denmark district contained 36 000 superfeet of timber.

The town of Pemberton, the so-called capital of the 'Kingdom of the Karri' is surrounded for hundreds of square kilometres by these forest giants. Although this is a great milling district, providing some of the best hard-wood timbers, some forest reserves, notably Warren and Beedelup, have been set aside to safeguard the species for all time.

The south-west is also the hub of life in Western Australia and the centre of population. Indeed, two-thirds of the State's 1 031 000 people live close to Perth, the capital. This rapidly growing city is a rare jewel in a gracious setting, built on the banks of the slow-moving Swan River and flanked by the white beaches of the Indian Ocean and the gently rolling Darling Range. Its Mediterranean climate, with an average eight hours sunlight a day and cool sea breezes, is the most agreeable of all State capitals.

The friendliness and hospitality of the people of Perth are more than tourist-brochure myths; life is attestably more leisurely here than in the eastern States. Everywhere there is evidence of the strong civic pride the 740 000 inhabitants have in the city's fine buildings, its historic landmarks, the broad reaches of the river speckled with yachts, the open-air music bowl, the beautiful university, the Narrows bridge, and King's Park, the pride of Perth, on Mt Eliza. Here, in spring, the natural bush is aflame with colour, the profusion of wildflowers matched by the flowering trees and shrubs, which include the unique kangaroo-paw, the State's floral emblem.

Not far away, only nineteen kilometres off the coast from the State's second city Freemantle, is the popular resort of Rottnest Island. This low-lying island, with its simple attractions of sun, surf and beaches, is well-known to naturalists and tourists for its population of rare marsupials, the quokkas. Dutch seamen who landed here in the 17th century mistook these small wallabies for

Fringing the desert, rocky gorges and bare iron mountains

rodents and gave the island its name, Rottnest: 'rat's nest'.

But if the south-west is in a sense the heart of Western Australia, its landscape is unrepresentative of this vast, largely uninhabited State. The West supports some of the most isolated settlements in the continent, dotted along the coast northwards and hanging tenuously to life on the fringes of the great central deserts which spill across the eastern border of the State like an encroaching sea of sand and sun-baked plains.

In places these wilderness areas are accessible to the venturesome traveller. On the coast at Eucla, about twenty-four kilometres from the South Australian border, massive shifting dunes form an ocean of sand which is both beautiful and terrifying. Not far away, the world's longest stretch of unbroken cliffs — 193 kilometres of them — occurs at the head of the Great Australian Bight. The saw-toothed cliffs, sixty to 120 metres high, are the abrupt termination of the Nullabor Plain as it meets the Southern Ocean. The great curving sweep of the coast which forms the Bight embraces much of southern South Australia and Western Australia. In the lee of its hostile shores which stretch for 1 609 kilometres, there is only one safe all-weather anchorage.

The monotonous plains near Esperance spill on to a coastline of wide, lonely beaches and rugged headlands, but Esperance's popularity as a summer holiday resort for the people of the interior is now overshadowed by its rising importance as the port for the nickel mines around Kalgoorlie and Norseman on the western margin of the Great Victoria Desert. These sunblighted mining towns are among the last outposts on the Eyre Highway which runs through the featureless Nullabor into South Australia.

The landscape of the West is largely hostile to Man, yet it has nevertheless yielded him vast riches. Earlier this century gold mining flourished at Kalgoorlie and Coolgardie on

some of the world's richest reefs. Today the gold has almost gone but a host of other valuable minerals are mined in its stead. And in the north-west, a new mining boom of surpassing wealth is under way; as a result, the names of Mt Tom Price, Mt Newman, Kambalda, Hamersley and Barrow Island appear almost daily in the finance pages of the world's press.

The Hamersley Ranges are mountains of ore, with some of the most startling colours to be found in mountain landscapes anywhere in Australia. Gorges cut deeply into the plateau like great sheer-sided, red gashes, and many of these contain springs or chains of rock pools with permanent water.

Looking at the age-old remnants of the Hamersleys, it is almost impossible to avoid thinking about the beginning of Time, for these ranges are almost as old as that. They are not as old as the land of Yilgarnia or the ancient island of Stuartiana, where the Kimberley Range stands now, but they were there long before there was anything living on this planet.

More than any other State of Australia the West has retained that free-and-easy yet adventurous spirit associated with the stereotyped image of the Australian. For many, both in Australia and overseas, it is one of the last new frontiers; a land at once intimidating and challenging; a land where fortunes may still be made.

And the West has another, more modest claim to fame. In 1697 the Dutch navigator and explorer, Willem de Vlamingh made a journey up the tidal estuary of the Swan River and saw, for the first time, a black swan.

The black swan is, appropriately, the official State emblem of Western Australia. Its numbers have been reduced since European settlement but it is in no danger of extinction. To the pioneers it was a beautiful paradox; today it remains an apt symbol of the New World, whose spirit still lives and flourishes in the West.

**Mts Toolbrunup and Hassell,
Stirling Range, Western Australia**

A drive through the Stirling Range provides
many scenes like this of huge fists of rock
thrusting up from the surface of the earth.
Although not as high as Bluff Knoll, Mt
Toolbrunup reaches 1 052 metres, and the
height of these rocky projections is
emphasised by the flatness of the
surrounding countryside. Most visitors to
this spectacular range are impressed not
only by the mountainous landscape but by
the carpet of spring wildflowers, many of
which are unique to this area.

**Western Australian Wildflowers,
Western Australia**

Australia's native vegetation includes a
wealth of the small flowering plants
commonly called wildflowers. There are
many thousands of species, some with wide
distribution and some endemic to particular
regions. Wildflowers flourish in poor sandy
soils all over the continent, particularly in
the 'wildflower State', Western Australia. At
least 2,000 species are endemic to the
heathlands of Western Australia, many of
which are distinguished by their brilliant
flowers.

**_Water splashing over the weir,
Pemberton, Western Australia_**

Pemberton, town of the 'Kingdom of the
Karri', is 340 kilometres south of Perth. The
small sawmilling town is in a valley between
hills covered with tall Karri eucalypts, where
some of the best areas have been preserved
in Warren National Park, Beedelup National
Park, Carey Park, Brockway Forest and Big
Brook Forest. The Lefroy Brook, tributary
of the Warren River, flows through
Pemberton, making fishing a popular
pastime. There are also hatcheries and
freshwater crayfish to attract the tourist.

**_Karri forest near Beedelup Falls,
Western Australia_**

The majestic Karri gums are the tallest
hardwood trees in Western Australia and,
together with the Mountain Ash of the
eastern states, are the tallest-growing trees in
the southern hemisphere. Apart from the
splendour of their appearance the Karri
trees are a valuable source of timber, since
their straight trunks can soar 50 metres
before dividing into branches. Unlike the
damp forests of the eastern regions, the
Karri forests are sparse in undergrowth, a
fact which enhances the height and
symmetry of these giants of the forest.

**Falls and pool on the Serpentine
River, Western Australia**

The Serpentine River rises in the Darling
Range south-east of Perth and flows north-
west to the Serpentine Falls. These Falls are
augmented by drainage channels from
Large Eye, Small Eye and Magenup
Swamps. Pipeline Dam, upstream of the
Falls, is the first stage of the Serpentine Dam
project, designed to provide the Perth
metropolitan water supply. The Falls are
formed when the River divides over a
sloping rock face, cascading to a deep pool
at its base.

**Pastoral scene, Porongurup   (Top)
Range, Western Australia**

This small mountain range 40 kilometres
north of Albany is a National Park whose
outstanding features are steep granite hills,
enormous boulders, bare granite domes and
sculptured rocks on the summits.

**Bluff Knoll, Stirling Range,   (Below)
Western Australia**

The flat lowlands surrounding the Stirling
Range provide ideal country for crops and
sheep grazing.

**Kwinana Freeway at night, Perth
Metropolitan Perth, Western Australia**

A modern highway with a sleek new bridge
across the Swan River near its estuary at
Fremantle now connects Perth with Kwinana,
a complex of heavy industrial plants which has
grown up on the shores of Cockburn Sound
over the last 20 years.
The lights of the bridge and the highway
are strikingly beautiful on a summer night.

**Fish-Hook Bay, Rottnest Island,
Western Australia**

A few kilometres off the coast of Western
Australia is Perth's holiday island of Rottnest
— a low-lying island which offers the simple
attractions of sun, sand and a rich marine
and land life. The early Dutch navigators
who named the island mistook its
population of rare quokka wallabies for
giant rats — hence the name, which means
'rats' nest'. Rottnest is only 19 kilometres
from Freemantle and is reached by ferry, or
plane from Perth. There are many small,
rocky inlets like this one to interest the
visitor.

Loop area in the Murchison River, Western Australia

Covering about 146 000 hectares, the Kalbarri National Park consists mainly of an elevated sand plain, split by a huge gorge carved by the Murchison River through the uptilted rim of the scarp. This spectacular canyon is more than 80 kilometres long. Its precipitous walls, in places brightly stained by mineral leaching, are up to 152 metres high. As tourism develops, Kalbarri will undoubtedly become one of the greatest scenic attractions in the West. The display of wildflowers on the plain is superb in spring and early summer.

The Hamersley Range, Western Australia

These iron mountains run roughly between the Robe River and the Robertson Range in the far-north of Western Australia. For nearly 483 kilometres across the desolate Pilbarra district stretch the spectacular, humpy hills made famous by the variety of colours reflected from their rock faces and the richness of their mineral deposits. Large quantities of high grade iron ore are now being exported from the Hamersleys exclusively for Japan. Asbestos and gold have also been found in the gorges which slice dramatically into this dry, colourful range of mountains.

The South-east

In the southern-eastern corner of the continent the tail of the Great Dividing Range turns westward into Victoria as it crosses the New South Wales border.

Like a worn down backbone, the mountain vertebrae diminish in size until they subside into mere hills near Bacchus Marsh, more than half way across Victoria.

On both sides of these southern highlands the headwaters of important rivers are fed by the melting snow each spring. On the westward slopes above Corryong, Australia's greatest river, the Murray, has its source. Here the icy waters begin the journey which will take them across the border of South Australia and into the Southern Ocean at Encounter Bay 2 590 kilometres away, forming, as they go, the physical and legal border between the States of Victoria and New South Wales.

On the eastward slopes shorter, swifter rivers bisect the coastal plain as they hurry to the Victorian coast: the Snowy, Tambo, Mitchell, Macalister, La Trobe, watering Australia's richest pasture lands — the fertile plains of Gippsland.

Water has shaped the landscape of the South-east. This is a cool green land, spreading out from heavily forested highlands to gently rolling hills and lowlands drained by numerous streams, many of which, like the Ovens, Goulburn and Campaspe, flow roughly northward to the Murray and its tributaries.

The streams of this region are the products of its highlands and, proportionately, the South-east of Australia, which includes the island State of Tasmania, is the most mountainous region of the continent. Unlike the ancient ranges of Central Australia, most of the southern highlands are accessible and many areas have become tourist centres.

One of Victoria's most spectacular peaks is the 1 720-metre Mount Buffalo, sitting on its isolated granite plateau in the national park that bears its name and providing sweeping panoramic views of Mount Feathertop, Mount Bogong and Mount Hotham, across the enchanting Bright Valley hundreds of metres below.

The Grampians of western Victoria have their own style of rugged beauty. Although the highest peak reaches only 1 167 metres, the steepness and isolation of these mountains make them look much higher than they are. From a distance, the range contrasts strongly with the predominant colouring of the plains from which they rise. First they appear as a vague blue outline, then as one approaches, they become intensely blue and purple — an exciting foil when seen apparently floating above the sea of golden-ripe wheat rippling before the north-westerly wind over the plains of the Wimmera.

South-westward, a chain of old volcanic craters extends across the rolling plains of Victoria's rich Western District to the south-eastern corner of South Australia. Their most remarkable feature is Mount Gambier, a volcanic cone which rises steeply for about 183 metres on the southern fringe of the city named after it. Within the main crater lie four small lakes, the most beautiful being the Blue Lake.

South Australia's most extensive mountain system, the Flinders Range, is a continuation of the Mount Lofty Range which runs past Adelaide's door. It is difficult to decide where one range ends and the other begins, but a rough division occurs about Port Pirie, north of which the ranges become higher and more rugged and the country progressively more arid.

The great eastern highlands which extend down through Victoria re-emerge across Bass Strait. On the southern edge of the fertile coastal belt of northern Tasmania rises the densely forested mountain barrier, of the Great Western Tiers, about 1 220 metres high. From the sea, it looks like an almost unbroken wall, but actually some parts of this fault-escarpment, like Quamby Bluff and Mount Roland, are higher, or detached from the main line.

Beyond lies the Central Plateau, like a table-top sloping gently to the south and clustered with lakes. Tasmania is the only

A cool green land of tall forest and rich pastures

State in Australia with truly generous and reliable rainfall; the predominantly westerly winds drop their moisture on the mountainous Central Plateau where the peaks reach over 1 500 metres above sea-level, and there it is conveniently stored in many old glacial lakes.

Intermingled with her rugged mountain scenery, Tasmania has stretches of countryside that show an almost English serenity. The oast-houses and hop-fields of the Derwent River, the picturesque orchards near New Norfolk, the hawthorn hedges and freestone walls, the patchwork of paddocks, deciduous old-world trees and soft green pastures all contribute to this effect.

On the shores of one of the quieter bays of the Tasman Peninsula, the major penal settlement of Port Arthur was established in 1830 and operated until 1877. By then, a large proportion of the 67 000 convicts transported from Britain had passed through its grim walls. The ruins of this settlement, now visited by thousands of people annually, remain as a reminder of the darkest days in Australia's history.

Nowhere is Australia's colonial and convict heritage better preserved than in Hobart, capital of Tasmania and the nation's second oldest city. Although the population has grown considerably, and modern, glass-walled office buildings have sprung up, an old-world charm still dominates this harbour city on the Derwent River.

The other major cities of the South-east saw little of the convict era. Adelaide, South Australia's capital, is a handsome city situated on the almost flat sweep of country between the Mount Lofty Range and the long, sandy beaches of St. Vincent's Gulf. Because it is surrounded by 688 hectares of parklands, gardens, sportsgrounds and lakes, and because its citizens like trees and gardens about their homes, it is a sprawling city. But it is by no means disorderly — in fact, carefully planned by a qualified surveyor, Colonel William Light. One of its most attractive features is Torrens Lake, a broad expanse of water more than one and a half kilometres long, formed behind a dam in the Torrens River. It is only a few hundred metres from the centre of the city, and divides the main commercial area from the business and residential area of North Adelaide. Elder Park beside the Torrens, is the venue for open-air art exhibitions, recitals and performances, given as part of the biennial Adelaide Festival of Arts, an international cultural event modelled after Britain's Edinburgh Festival.

The largest city in the South-east is Melbourne, Victoria's capital and the second largest city in Australia. With more than 2 500 000 people, Melbourne, on the Yarra River, is Australia's financial and fashion capital; many regard it also as the intellectual capital — it has produced more Australian Prime Ministers than any other city, is home to the greatest art collection in the Southern Hemisphere and the biggest department store. It is renowned among Australian capitals for its boulevards and tree-lined streets, fine architecture, shops and Australian Rules Football.

The city's character is also the product of such diverse ingredients as its range of fine restaurants, its electric tramway system, the exceptionally beautiful Botanic Gardens and its penchant for orchestral concerts, some of which are given in the Sidney Myer Music Bowl, an open-air auditorium set in green parklands on the slopes above the Yarra.

Modern Melbourne grew out of the gold rushes which brought thousands of would-be prospectors to the city and its neighboring coastal metropolis, Geelong, in the 1850s, and reminders of the gold boom are still to be found throughout the South-east. These range from dormant and abandoned shafts in the picturesque hills of Gippsland, to the important provincial cities of Bendigo and Ballarat in Central Victoria. Here, the wide tree-lined streets and the Victorian-era architecture of homes and buildings with verandahs adorned with cast-iron ornamentation, remain much as they were when gold production was at its peak.

*Autumn morning, Lake
Wendouree, Ballarat, Victoria*

Ballarat, 113 kilometres from
Melbourne, was proclaimed a town in
1852 at the height of the goldrush era.
It is now a city of cultural renown and
can boast some of the most magnificent
gardens in the State. The best of these
are found around the shores of Lake
Wendouree, which is a popular rowing
venue and provided the course for the
1956 Olympic Games in Melbourne.
The parklands which border the lake
are filled with huge deciduous trees,
landscaped gardens and beautiful
marble statuary.

Rugged, Western Grampians Range, Victoria

Discovered and named by Thomas Mitchell in 1836, the Grampians are the 'tail end' of the Great Dividing Range and run north-south for approximately 96 kilometres from Glenorchy to Dunkeld in Western Victoria. This wild, bold and austere mountain range rises in sharp contrast to the surrounding plains and is composed of sandstone and granite which have been worn away by wind and water to form dramatic rocky outcrops. From these peaks and jutting bluffs of weathered sandstone, the climber can look out over some of Australia's finest sheep pastures.

Mt Buffalo road approach, Victoria

Mt Buffalo, in the Australian Alps, is one of the favourite resorts of Victorian snow-seekers. The 1 721 metre peak rises above the isolated granite plateau of the Mt Buffalo National Park, 322 kilometres north-east of Melbourne, and is strewn with many tors and granite blocks, including a number of great balanced boulders. The Buffalo Gorge, with its precipitous walls of granite 244 metres high and about 805 metres in length, is one of the most striking features of the mountain. The entire plateau covers 35 square kilometres.

Golden flowers of Wattle, Acacia

Australia's national floral emblem is the Acacia, commonly known as wattle. There are more than 600 different species of this plant, ranging in size from straggly shrubs to small trees, and well distributed from the tropical Queensland to the cooler south. Wherever the wattle grows, its dense clusters of bright yellow blossom give a welcome splash of colour to the surrounding greens and browns of the bush.

River Red Gums, Flinders Range, South Australia

The Flinders Range presents some of the best mountain scenery in Australia. Matthew Flinders, after whom this range was named, first sighted the peaks in 1802. The Flinders are a continuation of the Mount Lofty Range which runs from near Adelaide to the head of the Spencer Gulf. Despite the aridity of the region, there is a surprising amount of vegetation. The giant River Red Gums of the Flinders were the favourite subject of the artist Hans Heysen. These gums are found only along watercourses, where the trees are able to survive long periods without rain.

*Mt Feathertop from Hotham
skifields, Victoria*

In winter the highest mountains in the
Australian Alps present scenes of
breathtaking beauty. Mt Feathertop,
reaching a height of 1 922 metres is the
giant of the Victorian Alps. Although
nearly bare of trees at the higher levels,
it stands surrounded by precipitous,
heavily-timbered country in a labyrinth
of mountains and valleys. Snow usually
covers the peak in autumn and remains
until early summer. Although it
provides excellent open skiing
conditions, the peak has not been
developed as a skiing resort, unlike Mt
Hotham, (foreground) 8 kilometres to
the south.

Yarra River, Melbourne,
Victoria

Second city of Australia and capital of
Victoria, Melbourne is a metropolis of
architectural inconsistencies, yet it has
dignity and beauty conferred by wide, tree-
lined streets and spacious public gardens.
Truly magnificent public domains were
established in wastelands on the margins of
the original settlement and a community
tradition of tree-planting and flower-
gardening was established. It is a city which
varies dramatically with the seasons. Fine
views of the city can be obtained from the
south bank of the Yarra River which reflects
the surrounding parklands and skyline.

Captain Cook's Cottage,   (Top)
Melbourne

The home and stable of Captain James
Cook's parents was moved to Melbourne's
Fitzroy Gardens in 1932 from Yorkshire, to
commemorate the city's centenary.

Elm Trees at Bright,   (Below)
Victoria

Deciduous European trees flourish in the
cool to mild climate of southern Australia,
and their autumn foliage enhances the parks
and plantations of many Victorian towns
and cities.

Ruins of historic church, Port Arthur, Tasmania

In a setting of rolling pasture lands and towering cliffs and capes the grim echoes of convict days live on in the stone ruins of Port Arthur, on the southern coast of Tasmania. The church, of which only the walls now stand, is regarded as one of the State's finest examples of colonial architecture. It was built in Gothic style but with a square tower, under the guidance of a convict James Blackburn, between 1836 and 1840. It was never named or consecrated because of two murders which took place during its construction.

Ruins of the Port Arthur Penal Settlement, Tasmania

Between 1830 and 1877 some 67,000 convicts, including children, were transported from Great Britain to Tasmania (then known as Van Diemen's Land) to serve their terms. Many did not survive to live as free men. Today, the ruins of Port Arthur, the main penal settlement, are visited by thousands of people annually. Shortly after the settlement was abandoned, two bushfires swept through and destroyed most of the buildings which once housed 10,000 convicts. But remains of the model prison, the turreted powder magazine and several other buildings still stand.

Cloud lifting over Mt Roland, Tasmania

The 1 231 metre Mt Roland lords over verdant, rolling pasture land in the north of the island. It forms part of the long, severed arm of the mainland Great Dividing Range, and a little further south, the mountain peaks of the Great Western Tiers rise to 1 433 metres. Mt Roland is only about 48 kilometres from the coast and the nearby Forth River flows across the rich coastal plain to enter Bass Strait a little to the west of the air and sea port of Devonport.

Historic convict bridge at Richmond, Tasmania

The beautiful, freestone Richmond Bridge was built in 1823 at the instigation of Governor Sorell. Designed by David Lamb, the bridge was built by convict labour, from stone quarried at nearby Butcher's Hill. Despite the saving on labour costs, engineering difficulties forced the total cost up to £20,000 — an exhorbitant amount for such works at the time. But Richmond Bridge was obviously designed and built well; its symmetrical arches still carrying traffic over the peaceful Coal River 26 kilometres from Hobart on the road to Port Arthur.

Night falls over Adelaide
Festival Centre, Adelaide

A view from Mount Osmond. South Australia's
capital is built on the narrow coastal plain between
the Gulf of Saint Vincent and the abruptly rising
Mount Lofty Ranges which command striking
panoramas of the city. On a clear evening street
lighting diffused by haze creates an exciting glow-
worm cave effect.

Situated on the curving banks of the Torrens River
is the famous Festival Centre, hub of Adelaide's
biennial festival. The city centre is completely
surrounded by parklands, with beautiful flower
beds, playgrounds and sports fields.

Tamar River near Launceston,
Tasmania

This 64 kilometre tidal estuary, formed at
Launceston by the junction of the North
and South Esk Rivers, flows north-west
through wool and fat lamb country to Port
Dalrymple. Sited on the banks of the Tamar,
Launceston is the air, sea and rail centre for
northern Tasmania and main port for Bass
Strait shipping. It was first settled in 1806,
officially became a town in 1824 and a city
in 1888. The first hydro-electric power
station in Australia was constructed here and
the city retains many charming buildings of
the colonial era.

Dragon's Jaws in the Grampians Range, Victoria

In the Grampians Range of Western Victoria, great tilted slabs of sandstone have been shaped by the elements into weird forms which project upwards or hang precariously over deep valleys. This uniquely beautiful mountain range lies in the general shape of a boomerang and many visitors are attracted here by the spring wildflowers and by such fascinating rock formations as the Grand Canyon, Great Stairway and Dragon's Jaws. Large sections of the range are held as Forest Reserves and in these areas many species of wildflowers have been catalogued.

Wilson's Promontory, Victoria   (Top)

Wilson's Promontory, thrusting into Bass Strait, is a mountainous peninsula where massive granite headlands shelter wide sandy beaches. It is one of Victoria's largest and most popular national parks.

Snow-capped peaks of Mt Anne, Tasmania   (Below)

Spectacular mountain landscapes like Mt Anne, where the Huon river rises, are almost commonplace in the rugged central highlands of Tasmania.

Apple Blossom time in the Huon Valley, Tasmania

This fertile valley, formed by the Huon River as it flows from the slopes of Mt Anne, is famous for its apples, and many orchards in the valley are over 100 years old. The annual Huon Valley Apple Festival is held in autumn.

Tasman Bridge and   *(Top)*
Mt Wellington, Hobart, Tasmania

This elegant bridge, now under repair, spans the Derwent on high columns, linking Hobart and the eastern suburbs.

The lights of Hobart from Mt Nelson, Tasmania

Although it is the second oldest city in Australia, Hobart seems less a capital than an old sea-port town. It spreads on the banks of the Derwent Estuary at the foot of the forest-clad Mt Wellington which forms a dominant backdrop to the city. The harbour is one of the world's finest and is accessible at any tide to the largest vessels. The ocean-going yachts of the famous Sydney to Hobart yacht race annually make use of these habour facilities. In the foreground, the circular tower of the Hobart casino complex rises above Wrest Point on Sandy Bay.

The Red Centre

No part of this continent is more 'Australian' than the Outback — that vast open hinterland which is virtually as it was a hundred, a thousand, or a million years ago. Perhaps this is because it seems to symbolise the challenge that its endless space, heat and lack of water presented to the pioneers generations ago.

The fact that Australia is the most urbanised country in the world, with over seventy per cent of its population living in cities and towns, presents a paradox, for many still like to think that the 'typical Australian' is a tall, lean stockman, and that the typical Australia is the wide open spaces of the inland.

This is not to say that the Outback is any less real today. The Northern Territory, Queensland and Western Australia each have cattle stations which are amongst the biggest in the world. These huge properties sprawl across the semi-arid hinterland which the author Mrs Aeneas Gunn called the Never Never. As large in area as mini-nations they are populated almost wholly by cattle. As many as 140 000 calves are branded annually on one station which employs a staff of about 125.

Many Australians have no conception of how people on the vast cattle stations of the interior live, the hardships they endure, albeit in the twentieth century, or the risks they take. Few city people could order the stores required by twenty people for several months and feel secure that nothing was missing. Here there is no corner store to call on; no baker, no grocer.

There are no schools either, so children receive their tuition by two-way radio from a teacher often hundreds of kilometres away. Settlers consult their doctor in like fashion. In emergencies flying ambulances collect patients from rough station airstrips — if they are available.

The modern frontiersmen who work these properties still live out the grim reality of the Australian legend. If they are away from the homestead they have to tend their horses, roll out their swags under the stars, boil a billy of tea and cook their own meal. The days are long, the heat, dust and flies unbearable. But there are still stout hearts in the Outback.

Stretching over 77 700 square kilometres of the Northern Territory east of Alice Springs and lapping over the Queensland and South Australian borders is the Simpson Desert — the 'Dead Heart' of Australia. The Simpson is Australia's most formidable desert, respected and feared by those who know it because of its size, its almost untraversable dunes, its searing heat and lack of water.

Viewed from the air it looks like a great sea in a heavy swell. Apricot-coloured sand dunes, six to sixty metres high, run parallel, following one upon the other as far as the eye can see in every direction without any relieving feature.

After heavy rains, immense volumes of water flow into the desert from the Todd, Hale and Hay rivers in the west, and the Mulligan and Diamantina in the east. But there is no inland sea, and zealous explorers who searched for one disappeared, like the flood waters themselves, beneath the desert sands.

Running east and west of Alice Springs, the town which legend and history have established as a place of adventure and hard living, is the MacDonnell Range. About a thousand million years ago, this range, lying in almost parallel ridges for about 322 kilometres, was probably 4 500 metres above sea level. Now, with the exception of a few peaks, the MacDonnells rise only 300 to 450 metres above the surrounding countryside.

Although these exceedingly hard quartzite mountains have been reduced to their present size by erosion, they are still wild and rugged. To watch the sun's rays spread over Mt Sonder in the western MacDonnells is to witness a pageant of changing colours. Turn away for a few moments and you will look back to find the hues magically altered. This is the place which, more than any other, was painted with such success by

Pre-historic landscapes echoing the Dawn of Time

Albert Namatjira, the full-blooded Aranda tribesman who achieved distinction with his watercolours recording the bold colours and perspectives of his native land.

Further north, in startling relief from the monotony of the plains between Alice Springs and Darwin, are the Devil's Marbles, one of the unique landforms that bring so many tourists to the Centre. Scattered over several square kilometres of country through which the Stuart highway passes, is a curious concentration of rounded granite boulders. They vary in size from about 30 cm to over 30 metres in circumference. Some are balanced precariously one on top of another and all are golden brown as if through long tanning in the hot sun; some are so rounded and so finely balanced that they can be rocked by hand, in spite of their immense size and weight. Their origin, though hard to comprehend, is prosaic. Granite, in spite of its hardness, often weathers unevenly, and the Devil's Marbles, far from being playthings of the gods, are monuments — the last remnants of a rocky mountain range long since gone.

The Centre is rich in such awe-inducing natural wonders, but the grand-daddy of them all, the virtual tourist trade mark of Central Australia, lies 483 kilometres southwest of Alice Springs. Ayers Rock is the greatest single piece of exposed rock on the earth's surface. It is a magnet that draws tourists from all parts of the world to marvel at its massive bulk: nearly 9.5 kilometres in circumference and more than 300 metres in height, it rises from a plain of drifting sand, spinifex grass and mulga.

From about 240 kilometres away it first becomes visible as a low purple mound; seen at close quarters, in the absence of anything in sight to indicate its scale, it is bewildering.

Through countless ages, the erosion of wind and water runoff (at infrequent intervals rain falls on the rock) have worn smooth its vertical strata and hollowed out some of its flanks, leaving great steep buttresses between the fissures. A lot of the rock's catchment flows into the twin ravines above Maggie Springs or Mutidjula, the most permenent water-hole around the base of the rock, and there is always enough water to sustain trees in the eastern fork, several pools in the rock and another at ground level.

Both Uluru, as the Aboriginals call Ayers Rock, and the ritual rock-hole upon it, are places of great importance to them. The name is derived from the word 'Ugulu' which appropriately, means 'sacred and permanent'. Every feature of the rock — its 60-metre long stone 'tail', the numerous caves, some with Aboriginal drawings, the water-holes, shelters and bluffs — each has particular significance to the Aboriginals.

One of the most important places on its surface is the source of Maggie Springs. Aboriginal legend says that the sacred water python place above the springs is the dwelling-place of the great Uluru snake. Should the Uluritdja people come to the springs and find them dry, they would call out to the great snake who, when disturbed, would disgorge water which would again flow down to fill the pools.

On the horizon to the west of Ayers Rock is Mount Olga, surely one of the most breath-takingly strange and colourful sights in the world. Unlike 'the rock' it is not a single stone, but a rough circle of enormous rounded granite monoliths, reaching 456 metres above the plain. The Aboriginals call it Katajutta, which means 'many heads'. Each 'head' is a smooth, jointless dome with sheer walls, and each is separated from its neighbors by chasms.

Because moisture is held here long after the surrounding countryside is desert-dry, there is a surprising variety of life, including numerous plants and such native animals as dingoes, wallabies and land shells.

Red is the predominant colour of Central Australia and in the last rays of the setting sun the rock faces of Mount Olga glow like near-molten metal. It is an eerie sight, characteristic of this region where man so often feels a transient intruder in Nature's realm.

Ayers Rock sunrise,
Northern Territory

**Sand dunes of the Simpson
Desert, Northern Territory**

This large area which seems to stretch to
infinity is made up of arid sandhill and
spinifex country. The curious thing about
these ridges of red sand is that they run in
parellel lines right across the desert for
about 161 kilometres. The Simpson Desert
was first sighted by Charles Sturt in 1845
and it covers an area of 145 000 square
kilometres. Because of the lack of vantage
points, the wonder, colour and magnitude
of this region can only really be appreciated
from the air.

**Mt Olga group from the air,
Northern Territory**

The Olgas is the name given to this cluster
of rounded massive rocks rising from the
spinifex plain. They are as dramatic and
vividly coloured as Ayers Rock, only lacking
the majesty of its bulk. The Olgas are yet
another fantastic landmark of the Centre,
formed by the cataclysms of another age and
are found 48 kilometres to the west of Ayers
Rock. The tallest of this group of huge
humps is Mt Olga itself which rises 546
metres above the oasis-like Valley of the
Winds running through the rock system.

Seemingly precarious Devil's Marbles, Northern Territory

These extraordinary granite residuals are a famous landform straddling the Stuart Highway about 97 kilometres south of Tennant Creek. Hundreds of gigantic rounded granite boulders, sometimes balanced on top of one another, are scattered in heaps which appear to have been hurled down by a giant hand. Granite often weathers into rounded shapes as exfoliation peels off layer after layer. Some of the boulders, however, have broken across lines of weakness called joints, while others remain precariously positioned on the top of a huge pile.

Ormiston Gorge and Mt Giles, Northern Territory

The MacDonnell Range in central Australia runs in several parallel ridges from east to west for about 322 kilometres, mostly to the west of Alice Springs. Although they rise for only about 300 to 450 metres above the surrounding plains, the MacDonnells exhibit an unusual amount of folding and there are dramatic gorges where rivers have cut a way through them. Ormiston is the greatest of these with its cliffs rising hundreds of metres from the clear still waters of the Finke River and its rock faces changing colour as the day advances.

Viking O'Neil
Penguin Books Australia Ltd,
487 Maroondah Highway, PO Box 257
Ringwood, Victoria 3134, Australia
Penguin Books Ltd,
Harmondsworth, Middlesex, England
Penguin Books,
40 West 23rd Street, New York, N.Y. 10010, U.S.A.
Penguin Books Canada Limited,
2801 John Street, Markham, Ontario, Canada L3R 1B4
Penguin Books (N.Z.) Ltd,
182-190 Wairau Road, Auckland 10, New Zealand

First published by Currey O'Neil Pty Ltd, 1975
Reprinted 1976, 1977, 1978, revised edition 1980
Published by Penguin Books Australia Ltd, 1987
Copyright © Robin Smith, 1975, 1980, 1987

Produced by Viking O'Neil,
56 Claremont Street, South Yarra, Victoria 3141, Australia
A Division of Penguin Books Australia Ltd

Typeset in Australia
Printed and bound in Hong Kong through Bookbuilders Pty Ltd

National Library of Australia
Cataloguing-in-Publication data:
Smith, Robin (Robin Vaughan Francis).
  The splendour of Australia.
  ISBN 0 670 90003 6.
  1. Australia – Description and travel – 1976 –
  Views. I. Title.
994.06'3'0222